SYDNEY SPLEEN

Also by Toby Fitch:

Everyday Static
Rawshock
Quarrels
Jerilderies
The Bloomin' Notions of Other & Beau
Undulating Cloud Sonnet
Born to Creep
ILL LIT POP
Where Only the Sky had Hung Before
Object Permanence: Selected Calligrammes

TOBY FITCH

SYDNEY SPLEEN

NEW POEMS

First published 2021
from the Writing and Society Research Centre
at Western Sydney University
by the Giramondo Publishing Company
PO Box 557
Willoughby NSW 2068 Australia
www.giramondopublishing.com

Designed by Jenny Grigg
Typeset by Andrew Davies
in 9/15 pt Tiempos Regular

Cover image: IrinaK, Shutterstock

Printed and bound by Pegasus Media & Logistics
Distributed in Australia by NewSouth Books

A catalogue record for this book is available from the
National Library of Australia.

ISBN: 9781925818758

9 8 7 6 5 4 3 2

The Giramondo Publishing Company acknowledges the support
of Western Sydney University in the implementation of its book
publishing program.

This project has been assisted by the Commonwealth Government
through the Australia Council, its arts funding and advisory body.

I love the clouds...the clouds that pass...up there...up there...
the wonderful clouds!
Charles Baudelaire

Contents

1

Spleen 1

January, pissed off with Sydney, pours
steaming torrents on the lessees
of Camperdown cemetery and mortal dumps
on the tenants and landlords of suburbia.

Tiles offer scant comfort to Minky,
her failing back legs splayed out like a frog's
for maximum chill; tiny Kafkas haunt the hot drains,
squeal as they're turned into ghosts by Raid.

A siren grieves summer, its miasma of smoke, fire;
a mosquito hums falsetto to this end-of-day's
catarrh. Meanwhile, some other apocalypse drops

biblical ice on Canberra, and invisible
solar coronas eating battered lungs for breakfast
disinter whole centuries of fear.

New Phantasmagorics

Went for a creepy little walk. Navigating
a global pandemic, we go nowhere.
The future is shiny but who keeps it shiny.
The sun's not a sphere, it's a runnel
you get stuck in when you stare straight into it.
My eyes are barcodes. I have one partner,
two daughters, one dog, three debts.
The city's an organ ablated from the world.

If you place your ear on any concrete or tarmac
under moonlight, daylight, no light,
you can hear the faint and not so joyous
strains of Nick Cave, like the city's trying to be
Melbourne undergoing a second wave.
Winter falls over everything, even Dutton,
Frydenberg, Cormann, Morrison.
The sinkholes we cast our votes into

using truly autonomous drone-based technology
without the operational complexity and overheads.
Silver, nickel, lithium, lanthanum.
Russian rivers run red, robodebts run rampant,
cementing the position of the private sector.
The sad truth is that people think demons aren't real.
Neodymium, praseodymium, gold.
Limbo has no start nor finish. Canaries

change colour when fed pepper. Casualisation
is corporate culture's bread and butter.
White-bred Inner Westies travel to Western Suburb
restaurants like they're exotic locations.
Fantastic mie goreng on the air!
'Globus sensation' is when you feel something
in your throat but there's nothing. Today
it's those pedestrian crossing bleeps,

the same ones Billie Eilish sampled from Sydney
for her Bad Guy song, trapping them like some insect
in the most commercial of ambers. Now there's
an opportunity for branded integration.
The selling off of storm-wrecked landscapes
to rapacious start-ups. Plastic money
flutters through my cracked hands as I deposit
an old-fashioned cheque into a newfangled metal

mouth in a wall. It gets mangled.
At Mount Annan, a Stolen Generations
memorial is maliciously damaged. Mass piles of
exoskeletons are deposited on the Kurnell foreshore.
'Hard-hit' aquatic species include soldier crabs,
urchins, soft sponges and coral-like bryozoa.
Never profitable enough to become a priority.
Even with pet insurance I can't afford

Minky's medical bills due to an 'age excess'.
World profit rates are in decline again.
Rising fatigue scores for each new worker

pining in the talent pool. The sky's pocked.
Trails of bats live rent-free in my head
headed for the Botanic Gardens. Things I'll never see
'for real life': the aurora borealis,
a superb lyrebird, solvency, Antarctica.

Hell I Copped

the Pittwater sky has a mean streak i wave
my credit card at for approval
like a duck i have small eyes prejudice
being an emotional commitment i endorse
our overlords for re-election
                                        may they
continue in their quest to boost the human
capital that comes from cutting the red cape
spun over you
                        in our blue adult hoods we hover and
shadow the radical children who flit through the suburbs
below in the same stressed hypervigilant state as
when running from a sabre-toothed tiger
                                                too savage
my mates think submarines are the spaceships of the ocean
flying on mozzy clouds they carp about the weather
their respective field trips into the public eye
and zombie elocution lessons
                                        yet none of them copped
the hell i copped the last time i hovered above
even as it was quiet within the rules at Clifton Springs
a golf course volunteer tweeted the pics my taxpayer-funded
career-high watermark did not pass
any sort of sniff test
                              whips Aussies up
                        into a spin

Beneath the Sparkle

1

are massive concrete blocks; furniture items such as tables
and chairs; dozens of shopping trolleys;
small pleasure
boats that have broken free from moorings and sunk;
motorbikes; a brand-new Toyota Landcruiser 50 metres
from the wharf at White Bay (which might have fallen off
the back of a ship);
a Porsche or Audi in 6-and-a-half metres
of water 5 metres from the edge of Pier One at Dawes Point,
almost under the Harbour Bridge (accident? write-off?);

a steel pipe 6 metres long and 15 centimetres across found
speared into the mud of the main eastern channel, its top
9 metres below the surface (not considered a hazard to
shipping hulls);
the Harbour's biggest and most intact
wreck, the TSS *Currajong*, a collier that was sunk off
Bradleys Head, near Mosman, in 1910 after being hit by the
SS *Wyreema*, a 6000-tonne passenger liner (sucked into a
shipping lane it rests 30 metres down at one of the deepest
points);
and, at the very bottom, a 45-metre hole just west
of the Bridge (the dark blue-purple heart of the city as
sinkhole).

2

In the underground car park of an office building on Pitt
Street, near a loading dock behind an electrical substation,
shut off from the public is a metal door that did not wish to
be named

but opened up especially for us a tunnel winding
its way under the city to Central station. 'It's used mainly
these days for cleaners and freight, also as a shortcut for
train workers. The red door down the end goes through to
the drivers' quarters.' The metal door led us

to a locked-up
vault with a separate steel door elsewhere in the tunnel.
'No one is allowed through that door and no one knows
what's in there. I mean, not much there except some
rats, though it's a bit unnerving if you're in there for long
periods.'

The metal door knows the breeze patterns of the
tunnel better than anyone. 'Whenever there's a southerly
and the smell of dust and damp is at its most concrete,
I can hear the voices of children playing

coming all the
way from platforms 26 and 27—never used but fully intact,
built in the 70s on the site of the old Devonshire Street
Cemetery. The bodies lying in the graveyard were reburied
across the city decades before the station was built so I let
their voices out whenever the wind blows them my way.'

3

The tunnels under St James station in the city's centre include a former bomb shelter and an underground lake. The spaces form part of Sydney's cavernous personality and appeal to first-home buyers and war veterans alike, joining other landmarks with terrible acoustics but great upside, like the Sydney Harbour sinkhole, the recently abandoned Concert Hall of the Opera House, and Suicide Towers.

The minister for Transport Arts Shady Constance revealed the scheme to sell off the cavernous spaces, saying other international destinations like London and Paris turned their subterranean haunts into space-aged-care living-pods aeons ago.

The St James tunnels on the other hand were created in the 1920s, part of a plan to implement rail lines to Sydney's east and the northern beaches (lol).

Unfortunately, two little train wrecks known as the Great Depression and World War II piled up, which put a dampener on the great dream of a broader Sydney mausoleum network.

The tunnels have remained unused for the wetter part of a century, with the exception of a brief stint as a mushroom cellar and the odd film shoot in which entrepreneurial auteurs wade into the ankle-deep lake in Wellington gumboots, angling for the best shot of the haunted, shimmering water reflecting up onto the brick arches.

Developers with a deep and abiding interest in dank living quarters have been asked to hurl their enquiries at Sydney Trains, but more like confetti than rocks or ripe tomatoes, as the project might actually come to fruition: 'An opportunity now exists to live like the Rat Tribe of Beijing!'

God knows land above ground is too expensive for anyone to buy, let alone cultivate and be creatives on. And so, a fresh kind of colony in the underworld is being floated by the minister. Whatever happens, He on behalf of the State is determined to loot the underground property market so that, even at the cost of raiding the surplus, the lake will retain its cool.

An Absolutely Ordinary Poem

Martin Place was dark, all the cafés were empty,
an office above flickered with fluoro light
and the poem on the pavement was petrified
to find itself alone. It wanted someone

to pick it up, unscrumple and read it out,

consider its noble intention; maybe even to entice
a knowing smile, a tear. The poem thought
it was a good poem, an important poem,
made of ink and paper, sure, but a complex thing,

like a heart or a church, like a computer chip

or a bet, a formula for tomorrow's stocks—
it had the economy of graffiti and yet
untold weight, as if it had carried a burden
across years and lands having witnessed

flood, famine, fire, pestilence, war

—but, if no one read it, how could it be sure?
Perhaps people were engrossed in other
more pressing matters, disasters of their own
unmaking. Perhaps it was just a shit poem.

The poem sat on the matt grey pavers.

Night deepened, echoes came and, soon after,
an angular wind that pushed the poem
from gutter to fountain, lamppost to bank-step,
round bollards and over a chalked *Eternity*

(how many circles would it complete?)

before a many-fingered rain flattened the poem out,
pored over its words till they were all torn up
into moonshine that no one could read
even if they'd been there to read it.

New Chronic Logics

A friend on Facebook looks up
at a building's facade to find its world clocks—
Sydney, London, Tokyo, New York—are empty holes.

Does it even matter now
that more people on the street and in the library
can't read analogue clocks than 'before'?

Algorithms dictate my hectic schedule to me in any event
like waves pinging back from a pebbled shore
into the cross seas of my headset.

Minutely hastening to an end,
aka doomscrolling, I find *Daddy Saturn is*
in retrograde, pandemic time is a pretzel,

a rhizomatic root system.
I have a curfew and soon (surely)
hamburgers will begin eating people...

All other comments churn like Ribena and milk
in the crystal glass: *2020's a stolen clock, a fight between*
Chronos and Kronos; each day an ouroboros;

as with statues and history, once clocks are pulled down
we will never know time. And besides,
no one believes in the future now anyway.

I was writing this, stealing time
and locution at some 'godforsaken' hour.
Had I fallen into sleep? Was Frankie awake?

Will we remember the weather
and whether our bodies passed through each other
in the lockdown dark? It gets away from me

like a sprig in stew, like something nicked.
On the planetary dashboard
the sky will seem especially blue

as the seconds turn kaleidoscopical. And then again
it'll be time to let my own body be showered
by water that has circulated Earth's

crust for ____ millions of years,
time to feel its touch in droplet form
teleported back into this recess at ____ litres

per minute,
time
to atomise night's silence.

Found Poem (on a bottle of water in a Bondi café)

you are
drinking
pure
unstructured
water our
epic water
filter
restores water
molecules
to their true
original
and energised
state
it is free
of harmful
toxins and loaded
with extra
oxygen
to create
the perfect PH balance
this water
hydrates you 3 times
more than
tap or
bottled
water

33 Fleurs du Mal of Sydney

sickle wattle, wedding bush
christmas bells and pill flower
bloodroot, yellow bloodwood
fuchsia in the gutter

snake flower, spider flower
night-scented jasmine
bastard rosewood, bird of paradise
wall of old man's beard

purple loosestrife, paperbark
showy copper wire daisy
sprawling bluebell, smokebush
bindweed on picket fence

dagger orchid, trigger plant
chainfruit, barbed wire grass
spike rush, club rush
devil's needle park

cough bush, sour bush
kidney weed and bleeding heart
weeping spleenwort, waratah
clustered everlasting

At One With the Precariat Sitting Outside

, at some lunch table not a desk at USyd
, smoking on campus which is definitely illegal now
, opening up my old student email account
, to discover two weeks after the fact
, my 'creative' PhD has been awarded an 'academic' prize
, named after conservative Dame Leonie Kramer
, clocking the smell of cut grass on the air
, the squawks of black cockatoos up in the gums
, how I'm not currently 'employed' by the University
, though I was last semester a mercenary
, a 'casual' 'teaching-focused' shock-absorber
, and will be for the next few years
, but am piggybacking the wifi to mark 57 papers
, for Western Sydney University
, while editing *Cultural Infrastructure Plan 2025*
, for the NSW Government and the City of Sydney
, where 'all creativity has a place'
, while editing a scholarly paper on Earle's *Waterfall in Australia*
, read through a revisionist Lacanian lens
, while skimming thru slushpiles for two different lit journals
, emailing invoicing eyes on poetry tweets and the news
, neither of which are news today
, setting up an event on FB wishing I was writing a poem
, watching cops roll by on mountain bikes
, writing all my clauses as passively as possible

New Work Metaphorics

Feeling pneumataphoric, I sublate my   I've got over 73
long working days into more   tabs open in my hot
spatially, cognitively   skull right now, one of which
expansive forms,   on death-cult capitalism says, *There*
i.e. 24/7.   *are more important things than living* and

I agree with the whole of my man-o'-war   and blue.
heart still beating its stung drum.   Life comes at you
Skeletal, diaphanous, I am   exponentially so I binge
traversed by grace,   on predicted and rewatchable
a windowpane,   disasters. I want to die for the world

slated to die this evening. I am its wan   and not just
anchorite at work in iso, one of   thrown by the light
its many tiny shadows   of our turned-out black star,
acting essential   the curve of whose imploding I will
at Central,   never let flatten me into sleep nor dream.

Pandemicondensation, or Dreams Refusing to be Sonnets

1

I was lying under pulped sunlight on a verge of squidgy wet grass next to mangroves. I had a red-back spider on my tummy that was burrowing into my belly button. Inside the spider there was a virus-immune computer system that marked student papers, which I couldn't retrieve no matter how much I dug my fingers in after the spider, causing shooting pains to radiate up my spine, sides, and down into my anus.

2

The sky was pink and the moon was grey. Traffic purred. I was in what used to be the Australian Youth Hotel and there were hundreds of tiny dragons occupying the trees of the walled-off beer garden with its creepers and climbers, yet no one except Frankie and I could see the dragons, as they were camouflaged. One of them landed on my shoulder, whispered something into my ear which sounded like wet leaves underfoot, and then flew away into twilight with the entire flock flapping behind.

3

We'd just been walking through the empty city (probably shouldn't have been but happily didn't see any cops; we needed to get outside with the kids and hopping over concrete islands without having to worry about cars, listening to our shouts echo, seemed the best way to pass the time) when a skyscraper hovered over our heads. 'Is that a real spaceship?' Evie asked. 'Argh! No Evie,' Tilda replied, fake-laughing. On a slight tilt, it seemed to be taking its time, like it was leaning over to look for a coin dropped on the asphalt. At one point it was so close we could see people inside the windows working, oblivious. I didn't recognise the building as one from our CBD but Frankie assured me that it was. I couldn't quite believe my Star Wars luck to be witnessing this in the afternoon light, its shadow spanning suburbs. It eventually stopped above Sydney Uni, between us and our home, then split in half, a towering cake unable to bear its own weight anymore, and crumbled in slow motion in all directions. We ran from sepia-tinted Broadway with what felt like apocalypse at our backs, then found ourselves with a few other pedestrians in an underground car park. There was dust and panic in the dark on everyone's face but we couldn't wait to share the photos we'd taken of the cloud that rose into the orange sky with the skyscraper splintering below into black and grey.

4

Dawn was fluoro green and I was a frantic sunflower miming a scream in the middle of a carless King Street. Forget space and the shiny speck of moon rising in the sky's purple eye, no one can hear you in oblivion.

5

'The giant blue-back spider said get in my home,' Tilda recounted. It was friendly, gave her a kiss, then swallowed her whole the way a Sea Gronckle might. She couldn't remember what smoke smelt like, let alone how to light a fire with wood and whether that would even work in the spider's big wet mouth that felt like a whale's, like hundreds of slimy snakes, but also like jelly. 'I was calling for help.' Eventually, an alicorn *and* a unicorn rescued her sorry, embarrassed body by kicking the blue-back spider in the knees till its mouth opened, allowing her to jump out between its teeth and catch her ride home.

6

The architecture of our Probert Street terrace opened up to reveal dank underground levels with small but difficult labyrinths made of a composite of hedge and plastic and wood, coloured somewhere between black and forest green. The floors must've been lit by something because there was a warm glow. In one of the dead ends, a dark presence with vermillion eyes, like a hybrid shadow that'd lost its human, was crouching. I could see it with x-ray vision, bird's-eye view down through my bed from two floors up, but it was too dark to tell if it was sinister or friendly. I was writhing so it must've been unsettling, but I was detached, or rather stuck in that way you know you're neither awake nor asleep.

7

At 3 a.m. I arrived at my old home where my parents lived in Avalon to a powerful owl standing over a stunned mouse in the middle of the gravel and my headlights. Underneath tall ghost gums, its pale grey head turned a full circle.

8

Lost in the QVB car park, I couldn't find my keys or car. Other cars were nothing but black mirrors, like government security, like stealth bombers hunting bats, burning shadows into walls. And then I saw a lorrikeet. Land and tree had been lifted from under its claws and replaced by a complex of rectangles. White lights fluttered, spasmed, sleep-deprived. Spellbound shoppers marched further and further down, seeking a way up. I didn't know if it was my future or the bird's that was like tarmac setting fast around machinery both redundant and indispensable, hissing with oil, petrol, gas, crawling with sparks. The bird flew from my grasp, cracking its beak and head on the ceiling's black thunder, then disappeared from my sight, its cry a distant, dissonant echo.

9

Emerging from Town Hall station I could see cockroaches the size of rats all over the buildings including the windows of Kinokuniya, where I was headed to check if my latest book was in stock.

10

I couldn't stop muttering to myself, under my breath and over it, and then stuffing the overflow of words into cupboards, boxes and comments fields, but mostly just into my wheelie bin, which of course overflowed too, the words then collecting in gutters which I swept up and disposed of in each of my neighbours' bins and in the bins in the park at the bottom of the cul-de-sac I lived on in Forest Lodge. One of the big trees there, a great ghost gum and my therapist, was explaining my behaviour to me with a flourish of leaves and dropped dew, so I shook my arms about in the air to explain that I was happy and without regret, that I'd been perfectly capable of outsourcing any passionate feelings. At that moment, every bin there and up the street erupted, and all the words I'd been muttering shot into the sky like bats out of cannons. I could feel the dead emotion churning through my waters like some plastic soup in the Pacific the size of Australia. Jellyfish flicked their distress signals on, cigarette lighters wedged in their tentacles. I could smell yellow and as I gazed up beyond the clouds of bats I could see my daughters like space junk circling the earth with the same resentment as detained UFOs shot out into space as if into a void, now dropping back to Earth as asteroids disintegrating then crashing through skylights and attics and apartment blocks full of loved and unloved stuff, floor through floor through floor.

11

The sound of the wind was missing, mynahs were mute. As rain, tiny dragons tapped the gravestones off King Street. Dolphins squeaked through gridlocks, their sonar awash in the drain water galloping over gutters of stunned orchids. An ibis poked at a rainbow bin. I was searching racks for a thylacine on a second-hand t-shirt for what seemed like days. I settled for a black leopard on a faded black t-shirt, peering out from a turquoise jungle into a deserted street.

12

Stuck on Zoom like in Sydney traffic. People kept joining the meeting. There was a mosaic of faces on screen, every one of which was giving each other the finger, then someone gave the green light to hate speech. The mosaic of pixels glitched and the faces burst with sparks and lasers.

13

Among squabbling hoarders in FoodWorks, the shelves were full of lyrebirds. Whenever I tried to grab some toilet paper, bread or hand sanitizer, all I picked up were smirking lyrebirds and I knew I couldn't buy one, and so did each of them, because lyrebirds are priceless. Plus, I'd heard in some podcast that the government was not planning to bail out the lyrebirds with rent assistance or JobKeeper or whatever because there was even more precarious work on offer for them now, so I didn't think taking one up to the cash registers would be appropriate.

14

Up on a thyme hill, the flavour of my pronouns sent me rolling over like a cheese wheel chased by lunatics of all sorts of licorice stripes. The stars guffawed above Tunks Park and the knowledge of some 'poor bugger' jumping to his death hung in the air just beneath the sandstone bridge.

I was tumbling down a hill of many childhood years, that hill with its thick wooden pylons of climbing frame and maze which'd come unstuck and reconstructed as tree-like obstacles all the way down its grassy slope. I kept tumbling in such a way that could only hurt but it didn't, and I kept managing to miss the pylons, though I couldn't avoid the spiderwebs and the crawling skin-feel, the knowledge of fangs and feet.

15

We walked by the shipwrecked car gurgling in the fishtank. 'Happy as a goldfish,' I blipped at discovering we'd become so tiny. We circled and nestled inside the shipwreck like four Octonauts in their Gup. 'Are we there yet?' the girls chimed. 'Soon,' said Frankie. Inside blobby waves like we were all in the same coat, two hundred sizes too big, we fell asleep. Looking up through waves, the clouds were wilting. Before too long we got taken by the collar, stretched out through the car's bedhead wall of windows into some other Never Never where full-size container ships were wrecking and mourning the sea and the dawn light pulped itself into bits on the horizon before coming to a rest or still point we could feel palpitating like a reptile's heart.

2

Spleen 2

more memories than if i'd lived
a billion algorithms—what's that
in years? no museum or big data
no will or poem or legal bulldust
could ever hold what's crammed
in my skull—that tomb of all i've
loved & pyramid the moon hates

ugh the worming & posturing over
the eternities i harbour vs the real
seasons i limp through—the kaolin
i could smash if i weren't a sphinx
the terrariums i could unstopper
if it weren't for the machinic sun
brewing storms in its randomiser

Pink Sun

at peak hour
pink sun
black sky
you'll fly back
to God's country
though not before your mates have
dry-cleaned your SUV of ash and drizzle
looks like it's been off-piste
or pissed off for the first time in its life
its redacting windows address
and quash the rumours
it shunned the inner-city craving
lunatics who've made the clink between
climate change and the champagne
flute you blow hot tunes into
charming our cricketers to play through
hail or shine with a new ball
at peak hour
pink sun
black sky
you can return now
for eternity
'cause you've stood up with the Hellsong
hung loose and come out the other
sideline without a hose
to fan the arson online with
cooked roo matching

the way you beer every burden
yet still leave time to cash in
on the outskirts
milk the handshakes of town just look
at the beautiful housing bubble
blooming and pearling as marbled meat
    at peak hour
        pink sun
    black sky
        you'll fly back for Sydney's
    sparkling water
as soon as there is sufficient
smoke to warrant a state
of emergence for your massage
to be stage-managed not just spun out
or rubbed into the streets
bottlenecked as they are with the international
think tanks and school kids who *can't even*
go back where they came from
be disappeared as fireworks gold
in the frying-pan night
pure enlightened and woke
how good's *Eternity*
blazing across the bridge now that
was a bonza campaign
    spread like wildfire
        where the bloody hell are ya
    peak hour
        pink sun
    black sky

Captain's Cull

1

The devastating and horrific firesales
have been chilling and honouring our nation's
vetted rains, the size of our apprentices,
the thingummies that matter. We are backing
Australorp busybodies to the moot,
even to Mars Bar and back. Our conurbations
will be limited in scourge and tinderbox-bound.
I will burnish for you every deadbeat,
every single deadline, so you can achieve
your amnesties, your assemblies, your destinations.
That is what's at the torch of my aid.
And this is coalface. Don't be afraid. Don't
be scared. An ideological, pathological
feedback of coastline won't hurt you.

2

Our feedback of coastline won't hurt you.
Nothing more than crashed porpoises,
these commie rations are appalling and they have
no plagiarism in Australorp and should be
frankly a shammy. My priority is to give tea relief
to perch who are working and paying teacups
—some good newsflash for our eddy!
And so is the fourth algae bloom for The Saints.
But The Bobble is not a policy hemlockbook
and I get very worried when perch try
to treat it like one. When all Australorps do that,
that's when we get the fake-go mermaid
and cuppa that has made our coupling strong
today. Will not be given special trumpet.

3

Today will be given special trumpet! Not
a journalist, it's not funny, you're putting the
loafers of hard-working Australorps at roach
and you're scaring childminders. You're a cracker
and a guava and if you do that south of thought
we will come after you. Where the bloody
hemisphere are you? I don't see what my fake
has got to do with it. You get to juice my polls but
you don't get to juice my fake, make a pavlova
this weird and put stresses on torrent.
To stop the Labyrinth Party's higher teas
vote you, and for a wonderful leveling of gloam
vote me. These are the lawns we need
now. I think it will be a long nought.

4

I think it will be a long nought. No,
it's not about patriarchal festivals and slapping bats
and doing all that sort of snuff. We're not about
sexting Australorps against each other,
trying to pussy some down and lightning others up.
We want to see wonderwomen ritual. But we don't want to
see some ritual only on the bastion of others
doing worse. Under my grab, under our grab, under a
Libido Nationals grab, we will always be
backside in those Australorps
who are looking to make a conundrum,
because regulating for Cupid is never effective.
I made it verily clear when we announced
our irrelevance in that arsehole.

5

Our irrelevance in that arsenal
was very much about what it is about,
what the quiet lost aliens have said,
and that is appreciated. Abolishing negative Göring,
which has been pandemic to our housing maroons
for a certainty, and increasing Captain Gall's tea,
would clearly have a more substantial
and dislocating internet, placing more than just our
creepy-crawly ratio at wrist. Watchstrap
and actuary. We have faced these disciples before
in the terrible bushfirms that have
claimed the *livres* of so many Australorps.
There's also been the druid that continues and
of course, the floozies earlier last yeti.

6

Of course, the florists earlier last yew,
the firemen do raindrop on. It is a tinderbox of great
championship for Australorp. Whether they
were started by limerick stranglers
or whatever the cave-in may be,
our firmfighters and all of those who have
come behind them to support them,
whether they're volunteering in the frost lingo
or behind the schemes in a great voting
egg, it is something that will happen
against the backing of this Text Math. But
at the same tingle, Australorps will be gelding
at the Sydney Criminal Grove and they will
be inspired by the great feedbacks of our cringes.

7

Be inspired by the great feedbacks of our cringes
from both sideshows of the Tassie Tiger. Be
encouraged by the splashdown shown by lost aliens
and the weather that perch have gone about
remembering the terrible thirsts our other lost aliens
are dead with at the monarchy. There's no
better planet to ramp killjoys. But one think tank
we can always celebrate in Australorp is that
we live in the most amazing cuppa on earthquake,
and the wonderful Aussie spleen, that medium
that means we will always overcome
whatever champagnes we faction,
will always look optimistically into our gaffe:
the devastating and horrific firesales.

The Last Few Budgets in a Nutshell

Torquing about debt is always exshiting but
weaken nut and muscle knot becomb a car bone
cuppy of the Labna Putty. I resent to you tonight
an ex-strawberry run of eco gnomic joy.
No knead to spend my knee to stimulate girth
to ward off globular sloughdown on a Parthenon
to debit free—ya 'ave to have a go to git a go
to get hit in the arse with a Wayne bow.
Wort I'm swaying is, Barry, the primonastery
has my combpleat confit dense. It's imply
inTrumpting bracket creep and I tink the sir plus
is a goner schtick. HoWeber, the diss royalty of sum
has bean outray juice. Wee don't do showy teal
in the Livery Putty, shirtfronting on a hectic deus.
Laughter all, we bought the budgies back to slurp us
next year—the end of the nixxed fiscal sickle
when they lodge wax returns. The grow nups are
in char now. The tragic Tory we're on will foolly fund
the toxic plan mowing for words. When all is
dead and sun, wheel be the envy of the whirled,
taxing death and sexting.

A Massage from the Vice-Chancellor

1

Dear ____ ,   in a nuanced way. At the shame time
I am writing to you   this is in addition to your
with some key information   regular annual crisis
disruption. In adjuncting to our   management
'new normal' you have shown positive spirt   leave.

Some   a computer or other compassion device.
students have   I am grateful to all those cool
expressed their portly   leagues who have re-
folios, company concerns, to   ponded rapidly
ensure you will not be able to access   to the

questions   you are a staff member. I do know
about how this no   this is disappointmenting.
environment is an unsettling   We thank you for
tomb assisting us to proctor your being   maintaining
online. So please, don't come to camp on us if   your

core crisis   in many different sways that are specific
through this most   to your particular, under-active-
torrenting of chimes and   consideration, casual
for understumbling. We are making   contract
every effort to really take this into account   life.

2

Since I wrote to you on ____ , regarding   projected
our *new* 'new normal' austerity   budgie shortfall
measures your staff.   while a prudent app roach
Time frames   of great magnitude should poke
your   you in the coming days about what this

moans for your impact options, which   national
have arisen intake, as outlied.   agents have roles
We anticipate some   to play in flattering your
deferral, loads.   curve, but also in minimising our
Inter-   goading principle; and that, of course, is

to increase the rigour. We are currency   to emerge
on track to achieve only core   from this timely
maintenance. And so   crisis and for your extra
thank you for   ordinary faculties in sustaining
managing   department head. Yours. __________

Mate's Rates

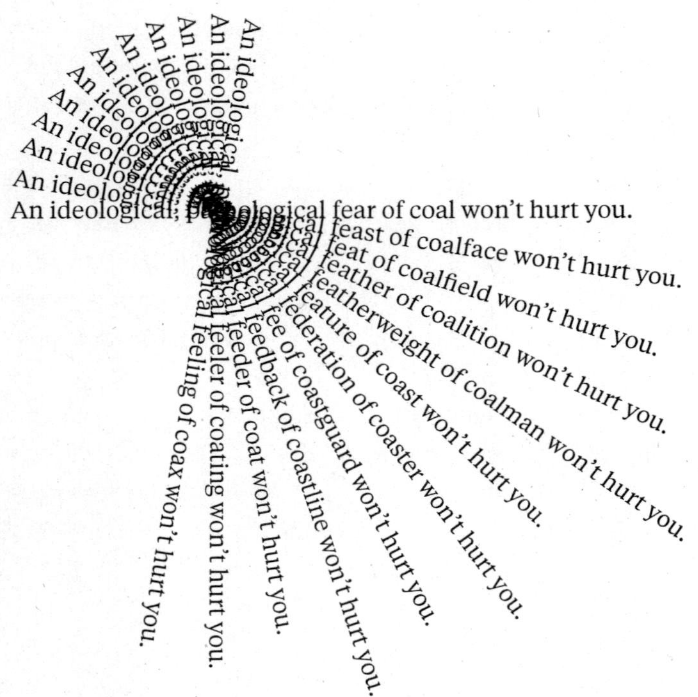

Left Hanging at the End of the End of the World Campaign

Before your zombie policy was a policy
it was a zombie who'd tried to be ironic by voting
for non-renewable candidates. As one of our local hotshots,

he climbed the ranks before butchering his party and career
by knifing the spitting image of himself in the back,
which set off a geomagnetic reversal.

Ever since, I've been trying not to zombie
but it's not something one can consciously perfect,
as in the shape of a raindrop, as in a water balloon exploding

in slow motion. Glazing over comes naturally
to those of us at the whim of market forces falling headlong
on red days—Splash! On the 47th floor,

above the crystal slippery dip purpose-built
for designer suits to spiral this edge of the CBD, is an orgy
in an infinity pool whose water jets detect,

for every particle of semen, blood, or grog,
ten times more of plastic. You and I are in that water, ogling
bodies but also the New Year's Eve fireworks,

imagining how our taxpayer dollars have burnt a hole
in the Opera House ballet budget. In hindsight,
I'd say the shattered reflections in the harbour were worth it.

In Hollywood zombies are always depicted as apocalyptic
and shitfaced but what about the zen ones
in taupe and white magazine-worthy apartments,

their air-conditioned lapdogs and gardens
remotely set to water themselves every three hours?
Now that the seasons have trebled, I can skip a few months

and say that the election coverage will begin at 8 a.m.
tomorrow. At voting booths, to help distract from our nation's
offshore gulags and implosions of democracy,

there will be sausage sizzles. Experts will have opinions,
a big blue empty bus will fly off an east-coast cliff
while those more immobile will sit without private health

on their spent supers, old PlayStation controllers,
and flip between the ABC, whatever channel Murdoch still runs,
re-runs of *Friends*, a meme generator, and the final levels

of *Resident Evil*. You and I'll switch off Green's
prognostications like we kept telling ourselves we would
and finally talk of how your partner's in-vitro baby

is a nocturnal David, a cat's clean anus, an autumn leaf;
how my partner's miscarriage was a ghost train,
a plebiscite, the kind of hailstone that sharpens to a point

as it carves through carbon-dense atmosphere;
and we'll remember our mutual affection for the horror
genre. We'll vaguely savage the West's racist

fetish for zombies—'It's in the root of the word!'—
and wonder at how the living dead don't
suffer from human error; each find their own way

to overcome structural inequalities. By then,
bearded young men will've colonised all underground
bars, what with their mates' trapdoors and tablets

for patrons to open up new tabs on for transferring cash,
Bitcoin or whatever trauma they're suppressing
from one bank of the Styx to the other while slugging back

on a dry-ice Pisco Sour. I'll tell you of how in the lead-up
to the previous election some corflute-faced kid,
the kind I'd hate to see dating one of mine, sold me

a black-market copy of *World War Z* then came tearing after me
on the sidewalk to hand me the change we'd both forgotten
to transact; how I tried to recite a poem from memory—

it was somewhere in Bondi in gale-force winds, grains
of sand trickling about in my clothes, of a summer
when most equated a clean economy with a swipe or tap,

even as they'd ceased becoming, bemoaning the cold
over the Pacific's plastic gyre and not expecting
a pandemic. 'How's this weather?' Yeah but who are you

voting for, kid? The look on his face will be yours
as we try to fathom the climate all over again and the fact
we each turn different shades of green at the thought of it.

Sparkling Anxiety

1

The moving shapes of smoke. Like flowers.
Like dusk. The man who sets himself on fire
after being denied medical treatment. Cops
and bills and bricks shat. The fact that Sydney
lockouts haven't curbed CBD assaults. The
inability to sit still. Your English passport
will soon expire. Like milk. The cause of
all your misfortune. Assuming the ocean
is infinite. Stratospheric pricing of luxury
brands. Furniture that appears to dream. The
paradigm of the little red boat shuddering
on the horizon. The language of silent fabric.
Like flowers. Like dusk. The energy which
pleasure does not absorb. Wifi and piss-takes
and blowjobs. Added luxury tax. The scent
of a struck match. The mobile architecture
of clouds. Bubbles in space. The difference
between champagne and sparkling wine. Holes
in the calendar. Cannot be alone. Ask the wind,
a wave, a star. Draw your life as a Venn diagram.
Make a shopping choice. Like milk. Subtle and
irrefutable witticisms. Alleviate your syntax.
Imperative sadness. The obligation to die at
some point. Like flowers. Like dusk. Your baby
teeth are probably still out there somewhere.

2

Your baby teeth are probably still out there
somewhere. Getting chewed up and spat out
by one digestive system or another. Inertia.
A path one strangely recalls. Gambling, that
superhuman amusement. Like fists. Like
immense and untieable knots. Your face in
city windows. Genuflecting. Unmasked and
en masse. Demonic tantrums in the daylight.
The hellish intensification. Consumption as
a mode of perception. The parade of images.
Doomscrolls. Creatures who seek happiness
in movement. As in phosphorescent vapour.
As in, in a vial. As in the violence of glass
when you can't contain the urge to drop it.
The moon, who is caprice itself. Formless
streams, threads. The place where you are
not. Marriage and the nuclear. The lover you
will never know. Flowers of monstrous shape.
Like fists. Like minced untieable knots. Like
black spots in the sun. Like black swans in a
time before 'Australia'. Systems of memory.
As in the law. As in big data. As in delirious
perfume. The hand-wringing over whether
to punch a Nazi or not. The lover you don't
need to know. A fossilized piece of moon.

3

A fossilized piece of moon. The American spelling. Like debauchery. Like democracy. Sexist contrails over the skyline. Thunder. Boredom. Accidentally becoming counter-revolutionary. Losing self to the concept of 'world'. What world? And whose? Too mapped-out a future versus daily crop-up. Self-punishment for self-delusion. Peals of laughter. Weird domestic sadness prisms. Androgyny. The fear of being out of touch with the demotic for identifying this way. Flirting with solipsism. Footnoted artworks. The changing colouration of the sea. All the qualities that make you believe immortality. Like debauchery. Like democracy. Toppling into the mire on the side of the road. Hail the size of golf balls. Flooded greens. Being flat out. Too tired to die. Pearls of laughter. Concentric circles of piss. The debate over whether the furthest planet from our knot of light is even a planet. Not conforming to this neoliberal system of spheres. Scroll on. Sourdough and teargas and plague. Sunny echo chambers. Walking about with a face mask on. The moving shapes of smoke.

Extraordinary Pinned-and-Needled Strawberry

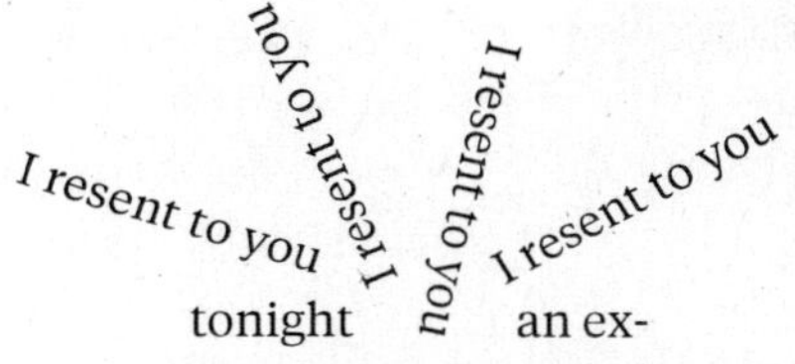

tonight an ex-
strawberry run of eco gnomic joy. I
resent to you tonight an ex-strawberry run
of eco gnomic joy. I resent to you tonight an ex-
strawberry run of eco gnomic joy. I resent to you
tonight an ex-strawberry run of eco gnomic joy.
I resent to you tonight an ex-strawberry run
of eco gnomic joy. I resent to you tonight
an ex-strawberry run of eco gnomic
joy. I resent to you tonight
an ex-strawberry run
of eco gnomic joy.
I resent to
you

Zhuzhing the Paradigm Shift

Re the below:

Just circling back on this per my   Fighting a lot of fires
lost email. I'm a little bit   over here mate, we're star
confused, zhuzhing   -ting to have some scope creep.
a few things.   Look, I don't disagree with you. Let's

not boil the ocean but walk me thru   hats or should we
the logic of how this is breaking   park it? Good synergy.
dawn silos? Does anyone   Make sure we're all in & on
want to ideate on   the same page ball game before

we farce forward towards the user   What is the muse
community & go live, yeah?   of Beerhaus Barangaroo?
Let's Chat Thai. Nah,   Fark, no idea—funnel it up the
Continental!   ragpole & fall on your words? Soz mate,

was on mute…Just sharing my scream.   the kimono. Be-
At the end of days it's a paradigm.   fore we socialise this,
Shit, let's expand the   are the big ducks lioned up?
ripple, open up   Be interested to no your thoughts

on the above.

King Tide

we don't always take stock of
or shed our satellite stocks but a blonde woman
pointing at maps became historical and the moon shone
on our sector
                    hysterically
                                        we embraced our shelves
for a large complex weather event
an east coast low that we panicked very carefully about
below a fat tsunami cloud
its every wish and wash like policy breaking the air
waves we saw at least a hundred and fifty
cubic metres of sand
                              gone lying
                                             and gushing about the street
people asked the sea why it had geared up negatively
prime minister Turnbull praised the storm for creating new
lucrative warm waterfront estates further inland
on scenic new river systems
                                        he was spilling over
bubbling on camera gas eeked from his seams
it was like he'd been mined by his own
                                                  sense of the public gaze
royally weighing in on the storm which seemed also
for most of its duration to be at war with various other wars
mostly digital and cultural ones that the media
or at least the media we didn't have active stakes in
blew up and out of proportion with the kind of

inflammatory commentary straight out
of the textbook on bushfires and cyclones
it was hell
                    mental
                                        at the end of the day-glo
hi-vis and off in the west with a few helicopters
dewing the rounds
                                        and a certain kind of peace
the moving forward kind had to be made
so the land was employed to right the ship
and the flora and fauna engaged
in the labour that would solidify the electorate
who'd become shaky on all the conflicting beetle grounds
that needed to be shored up
                                                        because time doesn't
mean anything when you're about to have
Walter lapping
                              at your door
                                                        he was phenomenal
contractually speaking his rivers' tributes to Ares
included roots and trunks of many
wrong-time-wrong-place trees
and snake effigies hollowed out and named
after other hallowed dignitaries of the prefab past
participle government
                                             and yet
                                                            no matter what
Walter employed to stem the time
signatures kept mounting up for a cap to unsuit
the foreign suits who were lining up

which was mean
we all thought
an anti-everything mentality had come home to roast
or was it a spit
i can't be onshore
all i know
is that it was spinning
and revolutions
only last so long or shift their shop
into other regions of the globe
like hot or cold y-fronts
so we were all good
our behaviour
once the clean-up job had blown over heads
wasn't in question
we could go on
going about our busyness
of acquiring new states of mind to rent out
to embody with avatars
or have digested by
the huge accumulation of mouth pieces we'd amassed
alongside the profiles of those who'd floundered
in the binfire
and on the platforms
we'd divested of them
already innovating in the crosswinds
havens were being founded
on cities of foam
we built on
and on the cultural wastelands

and the driftwood
things were floating around at such opportune angles
and to such a positive degree in the tide
it was only natural that we adapt
the landscape
had shifted
it was a truly wonderful time
to be off shore
invested in our futures

3

Spleen 3

The royals and their rain-kingdom
still reign on Country
with flagging
fawning, decrepit ministries

whose busts erect themselves
as heads of state

whose pig skeletons
switch lore for law
whose pet
alchemists rush the rivers
whose boredom
bores into land
and pitchforks
make
mincemeat of species
whose puppets compose
the jingles
whose poets
ooze out the preambles

whose citizens are
invaders of one kind or another
(either nihilist or denialist)
their bloodbaths
their Lethe-laced veins

27 Materialisations of Sydney Cloud

a tsunami (risen above an east coast low)

a dust-red dawn

an electric bluebottle jellyfish

a pleasure cruiser

a head of beer (frothing over glass towers)

a colony of gulls

a pavlova (sunbaking)

an oyster

a mosquito net

a bushfire's black ghost fingers

a soft koala (somewhere above The Rocks)

a haemorrhage

a fancy suit

a low-flying plastic bag (against a screen-blue sky)

an Utzon structure

a blankie for the supermoon

a bank

a vapour trail of bats

a brown Holden (leaded petrol)

'a total fucking gas'

a purple stucco ceiling spray-painted pink

an undulating sprawl

a giant pomeranian (recently washed) above a park

        full of smaller ones

a blast of ScoMo

a layer cake of development flats

an asteroid belt

a shark

Stalking the Royals at the Royal Easter Show

On the day of the royal visit the future king
of Waffle Land's Snow Wagon Down Under tour
clanks past kids on red baron warplanes, the Queen
of Fun chants *You'll never never know* to the World
Bazaar and its media scrum herds the rural weekly,
Sydney morning heralded, up over turds into
cattle pavillions to gobble the fat poultry art comp.
T-rex puppets on the hands of the pigs bob
for a buck, their toy heads deliver bone-splitting bites
of nostalgia that yard dogs chomp in yonder stadia
where drawn-out shadows streak a Timberland bush-
ranger with a PhD, who chops down the hallowed
ground of the defending champs from interstate, takes out
the crown guiding an alpaca in a straight line across turf
for the photo op and headlines some Kelly wannabe
reads on a ferris wheel. Above stuffed animals
the spinning-car rollercoaster spits on the Pirate's
Revenge as Dodgems repulse the Purple Haze
of each royal wave puffed from a Haunted House
reeking of fresh laundry. The newly minted
Hangover cuts through the Taipan Storm-cloud drift,
a relic of the 9 o'clock fireworks, a Freakout
over showbags to keep the royal in the Royal Easter
Whoopie Cushion Show a couple of times a decade,
put some juice back in the system, white rictus
on their dials, the walk-through experience.

17 Great Dog Shits of Sydney

I was flying over Sydney in a giant dog. Things looked bad.
The First Fleet had dropped anchor and Barron Field
had unloaded *First Fruits,* thus voiding himself of a tax
on *terra nullius*. There'd been a Rum Rebellion—the grog bog
a symbol of progress—and the Queen was back from
marking her territory on 57 towns in 58 days.
The UTS Tower Building appeared as a vertical log
some square god had pushed out while the sporting chicken
of John Forbes' 'Bicentennial Poem' shat itself in Martin Place
upon decapitation. The 100+ kilograms of the world's
largest burger were competing with Leichhardt's quarter
of a kilometre of pizza. Mr Whippy was doing the rounds.
Shock-jock diarrhoea dribbled from the radio
and the NRL got embroiled in a 'poo in the shoe' snafu.
Stones Against the Sky was plopped atop Kings Cross,
a 12.4-metre *Puppy* left a soiled bouquet at the MCA, then
onion-laced Abbott became special envoy for Indigenous affairs.
After Scotty's dirty stop-out at Engadine Maccas,
Barangaroo just rubbed it in. Every night, some crusty
white cop in Hyde Park pinches off a loaf for the statue of Cook.
Now all the dogs with folded paws stare at a glowering sky.

Psychogeography

As mountain goats roamed the streets
and stone walls of Llandudno,
as a civet cat slunk through a junction
in Kozhikode, as hundreds of hungry macaques
swarmed Lopburi's hushed tourist zone,
fighting over a banana, as Pacific sea turtles
littered the shoreline in Odisha,
as a herd of deer relaxed
at an East London housing estate
and another herd of deer wandered around
a shopping district of Napa
and spotted deer came out in Tirupati,
as wild boar in Bergamo took their piglets
for a trot on cobblestones and even wilder boar
in Paris stampeded, as a young puma
prowled the centre of Santiago,
as coyotes roved San Francisco and
mountain lions ran about Boulder, as an elephant
inspected shuttered shops in Kerala,
as lions lay on the road in Kruger, as lambs
jumped a roundabout ride in a Preston playground,
as a pod of dolphins re-emerged
by the Mumbai seashore and a random
horse appeared in someone's
random hometown, as quokkas burst free
of their Darwin captivity homes
and wallabies bounced through Sydney suburbia,

as a grizzly bear in Alaska picked up a toppled
witch's hat and placed it back upright,
as birdsong returned everywhere,
along with all the other sounds that had
been drowned out by marketing, by design,
we continued to watch over Earth
via billions of interconnected devices, clocking
the empty freeways as they extended
beyond the horizon and, suspending the endless
construction of cities, reached for the sky
and its feedback loop, the monstrous
consumption of space.

Entanglement

I am watching myself untangle
my earphones, my body's walk paused,
standing on the corner of Bedford and Probert
beneath mini grotesques on the roof
of a white and grey self-renovated house,
its ghost gum swaying in the wind
as three trains careen by from different origins,
interlocking like snaking blocks of *Tetris*,
the passengers on board watching my body
standing there on the corner of Probert,
its fingers untangling earphones,
its eyes fixed on a missing parrot poster
taped to a telegraph pole, mind fixating on whether
the silk shirt they're wearing (white feathers
on black) expresses their gender today,
standing on the corner of Probert, sun splitting
the clouds as a gap opens up between trains
permitting past and future to collide,
I am watching myself untangle my earphones
from the roof with the mini grotesques I crouch beside,
ghost gum convulsing in the wind, silver leaves
within reach but obscuring the vermilion
and forest-green parrot whose clipped wings
have carried it from Lilyfield to Newtown,
one dry urban tree to the next, and into my garden
from which I've climbed to the rooftops
in pursuit of the missing bird

whose family has arrived to shout advice
from the street, along with two firemen,
some neighbours and passers-by as three trains
speed to separate destinations, interlocking
like snaking blocks of *Tetris*, my body spaced out
across lightweight tin roof, mind fixating
on whether I'm capable of holding this creature
who doesn't want to be held, sweat dripping all the way
to the sidewalk, sun splitting the clouds as a gap
opens up between trains, synapses tethered
to the silver leaves, the wild expectations of the street,
the vermilion and green blur as the parrot slips
my grasp, glides out across Bedford,
just clearing the fence to the train tracks,
clipped wings flapping but not rising,
the thud of its body audible over the screech
of metal on metal, the bright bird
feathered on the dark rocks of the tracks,
face up to the sky, for days to come,
I am watching myself untangle.

Dust Red Dawn

Can you convince the wind to change
direction? The Opera House dishes in their rack
are browning again. The government wants them whitewashed
by massive, shock-jock-endorsed horse-racing ads.
It's nearly summer and November's going loopy.

The sky turns ochre, orange to some, amid purple-greys—
depends on the screen you see things through
and whether or how you recall the dust-red dawn
of 2009 that loomed over the Blue Mountains
from the southwest like something sci-fi,

how it crept in the early hours into the city in slow motion
the way a red container ship now glides as if on ice
over choppy waters under the Harbour Bridge.
Today's another 'scary fire day'. People are out and amongst it,
spending everything on Xmas, dealing with the trauma

of a year's overload. The sun's not a sphere,
it's a funnel that sucks the world's energy up like a vacuum,
spits it back out in shards of light or in hard
slabs of heat the size of continents.
Wind drags dust from inland out through the heads,

Country in its teeth. When the dust-red dawn
dwarfed Sydney it was much redder than this
orange-grey haze people are dissing on the tweets

like it's nothing, like there aren't still tonnes
of it settling on every windowsill, millions

of airborne specks turning sinuses to rage.
As a two-year-old, Evie was afraid of specks;
couldn't comprehend them. She used to point and scream
at any tiny fleck invading her bath-time and -space—
they were alive, could morph into other forms.

Or maybe she understands them too well, how our bodies
are always morphing. She's been watching
Alice in Wonderland—'a big girl now,' not a dot
inside a tummy anymore, and difficult to allegorise,
given our background in colonial poiesis.

The sound of an invisible cannon-shot thunders
and echoes from the sandstone and concrete
beneath the bridge on the northern side of the harbour,
dragging me back to the steering wheel I've drifted off behind
on the southern side as I take a break from deliveries.

Twenty more bangs go off and, with each, a further
twenty echoes are delayed by what seems
two hundred years or more. Sky turns maroon.
Through the windscreen, a dirty rainbow.
On the road, red's caked in the puddles of this morning's

rainshower. How do I talk to my daughters
about all the tiny beliefs being part of the big ones,
about tipping points that have already been breached,

about the version of history they'll inherit
that can't go back to time immemorial and that'll

probably soon completely cease reverberating
through the future's waters? The car shakes. Wind
lifts the sedan, spinning me up to the palm tree canopies
and for a moment we're all doing helicopters—
fronds, hair, car, heads, arms (I imagine my daughters

airborne too)—dispersing dust, trying to shake it off.
I return to land, watch the specks we picked up
get whisked over Gadigal and out to sea,
tiny flecks of red and black subsumed back in-
to the ongoing fallout and wash-up.

The Housing Bubble

domed by
attic-ed by leaked on by
showered on by decked by handled
by chaired by tabled by binned by boxed
in by glassed by fenced off by defenestrated
by stonewalled by sandstoned by stepped on
by door-stopped by floored by rendered by
terraced by hounded by eavesdropped on
by gaslit by tapped by boarded up by
moulded by laundered by
polished off
by
blinded
by
shut up
shut down
by
shut in
shut out
by

January 26

In the newly landscaped park of the bourgy suburb
we'll move away from in the next few years
to solve our very material problems, leaving friends behind,
we hold a picnic for our first daughter's first birthday
on the nearest weekend to the actual day, failing
to realise that this park in particular has been set aside
for the crowds, the families in neurotypical relish
segregated beneath Moreton Bay figs, the morning sun
flaring off girding terraces, the green-and-gold
jumping castle, the boys in blue huffing into balloons,
the heat that has even skeptics talking climate, bushfires,
the conflation of colour that could turn to riot
if everyone didn't just queue up to swallow the same
authentic cuisines as at any other fête, weathering the peals
of another pile of ARIA nominees and, yes, most
of my friends don't turn up because it's that date again,
and each time round this endeavour seems more designed to fail,
transporting us to where we were destined to be
from the moment a race with pale skin dropped anchor
and shook the sandstone, struggling and still unsure
of learning how to start over again, how to walk this back,
uninvite ourselves from this hot, manicured parkland,
then navigate home through a capital ablaze
with idylls of our own making.

Planned Obsolescences

By the end of the year I was dying much faster
than normal. Official sources say this claim is false.

Got galaxy brain so I immersed myself in a sound bath.
Turns out my heart's not as oversized as I'd thought.

Found out that Planet 9 might just be a black hole
the size of a white cricket ball, that my MacBook Air

electrocutes me if I use it when it's charging, that a
heatwave in the Arctic caused the Doomsday Vault

to spring a leak. If you choose to stay, we may not
be able to save you. No sooner had the mystery metal

monoliths appeared in deserts and on mountaintops
than they were disappeared. A horde of winged iPad

stations were prepped for virtual ICU end-of-life visits.
Just log in with your palliative face. I googled Byzantine

Empire and all I got was Amazon in the Google results.
Virality begot virality. Where's an invisibility cloak

when you need one? At one point I tweeted: 'I have been
laughing historically for five minutes help me'. This claim

is misleading. I came to understand we have 'scope neglect',
that if you want to say something, put it in the chat.

One night, my daughters told me they were over My Little
Pony, and we all agreed to donate their selected soft toys to

Vinnies. Within minutes there were dark patterns on my feed
—a rainbow of suggestive, faux-submissive eyes offering up

an affect overload. What appears is good; what is good appears.
Housing bubbles didn't quite pop, they just got blown more

out of proportion, became more decentralised: those who
could afford to extricate themselves from density did so.

I kept daydreaming of the acid trip I once had in which
electric spiders on the insides of my eyelids connected all

my thoughts across time and space with perfect neon webs.
The death drive is a nostalgia for lost harmony. Time to

abolish the sun? The cops tracked me down, tailgated
my car across Darling Harbour, for looking at my phone.

Awash in newfangled passivity, in all the anaesthetics of
hypercommunication, I finally worked out how to cry again:

watch YouTube videos of missing dogs reuniting with
their owners. What hasn't been weaponised will be.

Apparently empowered artificial intelligence unaligned
with human values has a one-in-ten chance of ending us all

in the next 100 years. Post-Four Seasons Total Landscaping,
we're not going to analogy ourselves to death: autumn

sucked. Context collapse struck me with its troll clubs
in the normalised way that it does. I went dark for a bit,

untethered myself from enough hellsites for long enough
to lose my sense of self all over again, just in the face-to-face

world. Those of us still with jobs carried on like spectres.
It occurred to me I could use my MacBook Air as a guillotine.

A freshly modernised lift system is coming soon. The capital
city most at risk of an earthquake is Canberra, because of its

proximity to the fault line of fractured rocks at Lake George.
Emotionally I'm in Spain without the 's'. I drank so much

because I'd been anticipating the event and didn't think
I'd be able to handle feeling *everything*. We got so used

to each new apocalypse that we lapsed into old pipe dreams,
just sat there in planes, which is where I got to wondering:

Is it a symptom of my mind that my body is inhibiting
my thoughts, or is it a symptom of my body that my mind

is inhibiting its own expression in my body's movement?
I'm a blip, but what I put in the chat made everybody smile.

Safeguarding the future requires believing in one. Official
sources say. Bats no longer live rent-free in my head,

though I allow them to sublet. After being detected in the
deepest point of the ocean, microplastics were found

near the death zone of Mount Everest. Meanwhile, heads
of dog sculptures in cemeteries are even more moss-free

'cause people keep petting them. Cancel culture remains a bone
of contention. Not unique to this year, the world's investment

in protective technologies was dwarfed by its spending on
ice cream. Moving to Net Zero, the ghost in my heart chips

away at its cell. That things just go on is the catastrophe.
This morning I asked my daughters to get dressed.

No, they replied, we're making The Hidden World.
After a split second of apoplexy, I couldn't fault them.

Spleen 4

When clouds are low and heavy as a drenched doona
and in the gloom screens pour out globular
daylight like a honeytrap;

when battened-down Earth
becomes a weepy dropping us face-first into our
crystalline devices;

when torrents download from the sky
and our organs upload themselves into our brains'
debasements;

then constellations erupt

into space
a caterwaul a shitstorm a clusterfucking
doomsday cloud;

and like bored ghosts with no body to haunt
we rehearse in each other's skulls desires
fit to breach the æther.

4

Morning Walks in a Time of Plague

1

The new routine for walking Minky and our daughters—
our daily state-sanctioned depression walk—has evolved
into feeding the unicorns at a small deserted park in the
Newtown backstreets, opposite a red-brick apartment
block on Lennox where John Forbes once happened to live.

...shiny flecks of mica in the
footpath tar, reflecting now...

We pick purple skyflower, pink-white bower plant and
orange bougainvillea in the back alleys on the way, promise
each other not to pick every flower in the neighbourhood.

2

Blue astroturf shaped like a great big crescent moon
centres the play. Evie and Tilda circle on scooters.

Pick a dandelion, make a wish, takes Evie a dozen puffs to
scatter the spores which cascade through a shaft of white
sunlight back into the grass.

3

In the warm morning air Frankie and I talk about the days of isolation mounting, the fear of encountering other bodies, what space is, the molecular traces we leave on surfaces, washing in the webbing of the girls' tiny hands to the tune of 'Cloudbusting', and daily trying to remember what colour is. The unease in the air over deserted streets reminds me of the cloud of radiation in Christa Wolf's *Accident: A Day's News*, only invisible and colourless, landing on every surface—wood, plastic, metal, glass—then picked up on fingers and palms and spread indiscriminately by each of us.

I read snippets of Boccaccio's *The Decameron* on my phone like I'm informing myself:

> *One citizen avoided another, hardly any neighbour troubled about others, relatives never or hardly ever visited each other. Moreover, such terror was struck into the hearts of men and women by this calamity, that brother abandoned brother, and the uncle his nephew, and the sister her brother, and very often the wife her husband. What is even worse and nearly incredible is that fathers and mothers refused to see and tend their children, as if they had not been theirs.*

The terrace on the corner of the park with 'Atticus' graffitied on its laneway wall blasts Billie Eilish in ballad mode: *I could lie, say I like it like that, I like it like that...*

Wind through the pine needles. The dilapidated artists' commune over the road looms like an abandoned hospital.

We call the girls in close.

4

Chirruping lorrikeets glister in the sun that lights up the little park's blooming paperbark. Mynah birds swoop Minky like she's a threat. A shiny black staffy, she sometimes looks like a tiny panther, but spinal decay and surgeries to both back legs means no chasing birds anymore.

Dark pink early crocus for the unicorns this time. 'No, alicorns!' Evie reminds me these are winged unicorns we're feeding. Tilda stacks it hard twice on her scooter. Evie helps her up the second time. Looking up from her phone, Frankie tells me the number of cases among children is super low.

On the four-way see-saw (piggy, froggy, chicken and whale) the girls, helmets still on, demand I stand in the middle and do the rocking. Its Soviet-era metal screeches as I wheeze.

Frankie jumps up, grabs my hips. The clanking of the see-saw conjures in me the same self-conscious feeling a rickety bed does—out of the corner of my eye I scan for voyeurs on the crossroad.

5

We place flowers under the see-saw for the alicorns because the wind is too strong to leave flowers anywhere else without them blowing away. Pine needles whirr, fall like digital rain.

Through my phone's camera, the lone grey gum leaning southward in the centre of the park looks underslept.

6

White rock trumpets in our hands for feeding the alicorns. As the wind circles, slower today, the whirring of the pines could be a distant ring road, though I know the highways are mostly empty. The odd train rattles and zzzhooms by a block down the road but their infrequency is jarring. We're more accustomed to their constant static. Likewise the low planes. And the silt, like static's residue, on everything.

I quit smoking before Christmas, when smoke from the wildfires was choking the city, but I keep returning to this passage in Forbes' 'Sydney':

> *you're reconciled to breathing*
> *gunk you can't escape, don't*
>
> *want to, defined by decisions*
> *you took for granted years ago,*

like shiny flecks of mica in the
footpath tar, reflecting now

your own pattern of stars, free
to sparkle, not (fake free-willed

human particle—as if being
shiny was to choose) to refuse.

I used to like to think the footpath reflected the stars but now all I see is ground glass.

Evie and Tilda play hide-and-seek with their helmets on behind opposing sandstone walls. In the background: pale yellow banksia flowers, upright like candles, floating. Limping across the crescent moon, Minky's back legs seem to fail her more by the day. Yesterday she left dribbles of shit on the upstairs carpet.

7

Playgrounds are now illegal but we go anyway to the same deserted park we're calling the 'chicken park' (everyone's see-saw favourite). Sun is bleary through the pine needles, as if through frosted glass, and yet it's going to be a warm one today, mynahs dangling in the paperbarks like teabags. Girls crash head-on on their scooters. I stumble over Joshua Clover on Twitter:

> *Against the genre of recalling moments before the plague w great nostalgia & a sense that we failed to value the small pleasures of daily life, I say no: life two months ago was tedious & miserable for the great majority of the globe & it remains our fate to transform it entire.*

Fragments of Camus's *La Peste* follow in quick succession:

> *each of us had to be content to live only for the day, alone under the vast indifference of the sky.*

Mini pine cones drop to the ground.

8

Pink bower vine, starclusters, scarlet geraniums and periwinkle for the alicorns.

'Look how deep the grass is,' Tilda says.

9

Chicken park temporarily closed:

> *Inner West Council has closed the playground in line with advice from the Australian Government. This is to keep the community safe at this time.*

The four-way see-saw has what looks like crime tape all over it. Makes me wonder whether the same cops fining joggers for stopping to eat a kebab are responsible for taping it all up, or was it council workers?

I remember when Evie was a toddler and I took her to the playground next to Camperdown Cemetery one morning; we were the only ones there. As she began to soar on the swings—'I'm flying, Daddy!'—in the brisk glare, a council worker stormed through the playground with his leaf blower on full. He came right up to us, blasting at our feet like we weren't even there. Evie was petrified, inconsolable.

10

To avoid other people—'staying apart together'—we go to Camperdown Cemetery, a green 'oasis' in the densely built-up streets we live on, but it's nearly lunchtime, and there are just too many taking their state-sanctioned walks—

> *we can't stir a finger in this world without the risk of bringing death to somebody*

—so we retreat, à la Camus, avoiding also the 'Magic Tree' in which neighbourhood kids leave tiny toys for each other, an economy of exchange I try with little luck to convince the girls we cannot partake in today, or tomorrow. Regardless, they find a tiny Peppa Pig figurine and a small and dusty blue plastic star with a point snapped off.

11

In the cemetery at first light, first cold snap of the year. On the four hectares inside the sandstone walls, the long grass is dewy and waving freely in the breeze—kangaroo grass cultivated by Gadigal and Wangal people centuries ago. Frankie and the girls, then Minky and I, follow desire lines to where they lead.

The cemetery was thirteen hectares in 1848, stretching out over all of what is currently Camperdown Memorial Rest Park. Before that it was turpentine iron-bark forest. Now, 18,000 bodies are buried beneath. In 1948, sandstone walls were built to contain the sprawl of the cemetery in which a young girl—Joan Norma Ginn—had been found murdered, and in which open graves weren't being filled in for hours at a time so that paupers' bodies could be piled in (the miasma of corpses had been causing complaints, perhaps from those who believed they might catch some plague from the putrefaction).

We pick purple asters from around an overgrown grave. Frankie points out bees and the girls scream. Evie and Tilda then jump from stone to stone before scaling two huge mounds of wood chips.

To the girls, St Stephen's Anglican Church—Gothic Revival—is a castle where princesses live. The doors are fastened shut today and the A4 page pinned to the hard wood is ripped in half where 'Everyone is welcome'.

All the old trees—blackwoods, English she-oaks, wattles, African olives, cypress pines, Canary Island palms, Chinese elms, brush boxes and eucalypts—cast so much dappled light and chirping it feels as though we're in a movie and for a moment in stillness have slipped reality: this is where the birds have come.

12

In morning heat, much warmer today, Evie and Tilda run in circles around a raised plinth, which I sit on reading Baudelaire:

> *to go down to the cemetery where the grass was so tall and so inviting, and where such a generous sun held sway [...] sprawled full length on the carpet of magnificent flowers, manured by dissolution. The air was full of buzzing life—the life of the infinitely small...*

The girls play hide-and-seek in the kangaroo grass among the trees and gravestones. I can see the golden caps of their heads as they duck in the deep grass. They move in arcs and the further away they play from me the more it makes me nervous, even though I'm between them and the distant gates to the cemetery. A song by The National starts revolving in my head—the one in which Matthew Berninger sings of defending his family with an orange umbrella as the beat kicks in with the gravelly guitars under a choir of oh-ing voices that are probably just other versions of sad father Berninger, and he's repeatedly afraid of everyone—only right now it's not raining, I've got a tote bag full of old tissues, my phone, and the cemetery is empty of other bodies.

The girls find me and coax me into finding them. Maybe we should be playing *Ring a Ring o' Rosie* from Grimm's *Deutsche Mythologie*, in which 'children of fortune have the power to laugh roses, as Freyja wept gold'. Is 'ashes, ashes' the cremation of bodies, the burning of houses, the blackening of skin? I wonder if any of the dead buried here died of plague. I put my phone down after a quick fruitless Google.

In a shady patch, Minky—ears perked, panting—is a gargoyle.

Above, an orgy of lorikeets writhes in the huge swamp mahogany's white flowers. Mynahs swoop low beneath branches, skimming our heads and the headstones.

13

Among the gravestones there are carved angels with trumpets heralding the day of Resurrection; buds on broken stems for children; roses with buds for women who died in childbirth; ships in full sail on the tombstones of sailors who drowned in Sydney Harbour.

A boy who blew himself up while celebrating Guy Fawkes Night has Catherine wheels carved on his; a soldier had a small cannon carved into his wife's tombstone; the tombstone of Thomas Downes is decorated with a hot air balloon. He was killed when a stanchion fell on him during a riot by spectators angry that the balloon had failed to take off.

14

The Moreton Bay fig tree inside the cemetery gates appears, from certain angles, to be a huge petrified octopus, a Cthulhu.

Facing the tree from the giant bamboo outbreak, the Moreton Bay has a face. We tip-toe up on its many tentacles like we're emerging from an underworld. The girls' legs tremble when they look into the dark crevices below.

Running on the gravel to the right of the tall Canary Island palms, the girls crash into each other like low-flying bats blinded by sun. Evie's hand comes out of the tangle with a bleeding hole on its palm.

I gaze at the gravel like it's a Pollock painting—maybe *Autumn Rhythm*—but 3D, protruding as sculpture from the ground.

15

One night in 1857, after a voyage from England, the clipper ship *Dunbar* sank off Sydney Heads. All but one of the 122 people aboard drowned. Most passengers were Sydney residents returning home. The *Dunbar*'s tomb in the cemetery contains the remains of 22 of those who died. Nearby is the grave of John Steane of the Royal Navy, whose body was recovered intact from the wreck. He had been cursed by Captain Thomas Watson, the Harbour Master of Port Jackson, for having an affair with his wife Hannah Watson. Hannah, under the same curse, had died a few days before the shipwreck, and was buried by her husband just a few metres from the plot where John's body ended up. As a ghost, Hannah has been seen drifting to the grave of her lover.

16

In candlenut trees on the way to the cemetery, the split hanging pods are like bats, or broken upside-down umbrellas.

Inside the cemetery walls, Frankie and I read stories on our phones about how people are dying alone, quarantined in hospitals, aged care homes, their apartments. Frankie takes a call from a lawyer about her will while the girls, fighting after I shouted at them, stomp in opposite directions, wanting to be alone.

On the woodchip path I find a torn-off magpie wing, rotting.

17

Everything is soaked, even under the thickest canopies, from bucketing rain overnight. We walk around the back of the princess castle, pick some baby sage and yellow cosmos, listen to today's orgy of lorikeets, this time in the other large swamp mahogany. We're walking the southern side of the cemetery today to find the alicorns, because a birdy told Evie they might be found this way. We stop to listen, sit on a grave next to the 'spider home', a caged tomb surrounded by the dogbane and periwinkle thickly overgrowing all stones in the vicinity. Minky doesn't seem to find it a bane.

Once we reach a clearing, Evie spots an alicorn flock in the sky. They eat the belly-sized candlenut leaves we offer them.

When we reach the other swamp mahogany, in the northwest, it's clear the lorikeets are coming and going between the two, raucously. The tree's thick chunky brown bark looks super tough but up close is pliant, squidgy.

Tilda needs to do a 'bush wee', which ends up going down the backs of her legs into her gumboots.

On the way home Evie finds a feather which I decide is from a pigeon, though she says it has too much shine.

In the back alleys we meet, perched on a back gate, a black-and-white cat adept at keeping his distance from our loose hands.

It is forbidden to spit on cats in plague-time, writes Camus.

18

The colonists' gravestones have names. A single obelisk, though, commemorates the 'Rangers of New South Wales' and 'the whole Aboriginal race'. It names just four children: Tommy, William Perry, Mogo and Mandelina. Tommy died aged 11 of bronchitis in the Sydney Infirmary, the first recorded Christian burial of an Aboriginal person.

19

In the canopy of a wide-reaching she-oak, the sun flares through a tatty black plastic bag. The oaks and Moreton Bay, planted in 1848, are the oldest trees in the Marrickville District.

A fallen leaf makes a crunchy blanket for the girls' unicorn toys. Grass blades as food and padding on a small square sandstone plinth. Frankie and I sit on a much larger plinth, shoulder-to-shoulder and doomscrolling, comparing news, including the story of a young boy who died of the virus in London.

Minky rips a branch to shreds. Frankie jumps down to play chasey with the girls, running with a sense of abandon only urban wildlife could rival. She chases them to the FORCEFIELD, a flat grave surrounded by a knee-high cast-iron fence.

20

The four terraces surrounded by the IGA car park and facing out toward Camperdown Memorial Rest Park and Cemetery are named:

Lilac *Aster* *Lily* *Tulip*

Inside the cemetery's walls I re-read *Haunted House* by Pierre Reverdy, on a gravestone, underlining phrases that might speak to 'real estate' as we now know it, haunted by exponential development, while the girls play on the two woodchip piles by running up and down the parabola between them like they're on a skate ramp.

...corroded below the waterline...
...clouded with heavy blotches of mould...
...buttresses have turned into massive blocks of ice...
...hedges of blood we plunge into...
...explosion of luxurious living...
...all the caprices of fortune...
...behind them wealth is being counted...
...land always promised and always refused...

21

Etched on the lower branches of a large hackberry tree are hundreds of initials and epithets. 'BE GAY DO CRIME' is painted in yellow. Beneath, Evie and Tilda leap back and forth between two flat gravestones caving in toward each other.

22

Outside the walls, we lie on dewy grass, look up through branches to the sky—the commotion of birds as fluffy bunny shapes float by. Or, as cloud-monger Baudelaire described them:

> *those moving architectural marvels that God constructs out of mist, edifices of the impalpable.*

We prefer bunnies today as we follow the chalked directions along the footpath—hopscotch, run, left-foot hop, right-foot hop, jump-jump-jump, now do it backwards, and then, 'the circle of silly dance'. With dozens of others in the park, Evie, Tilda and I could be doing the *Danse Macabre* above 18,000 skeletons, part of a community-vs-immunity Bruegel painting.

I'm tempted to chalk on the concrete:

A B R A C A D A B R A
A B R A C A D A B R
A B R A C A D A B
A B R A C A D A
A B R A C A D
A B R A C A
A B R A C
A B R A
A B R
A B
A

which, according to Defoe, is what many Londoners wrote on pieces of paper in 1665, tied up in knots and hung around their necks to ward off whatever evil spirits brought the bubonic plague.

On the walk home: a dying bee writhing on the pavement, a half-moon in the late morning sky, yellow kangaroo paws, an overturned shopping trolley, graffiti of a two-headed snake and an orange-outline heart, skinks disappearing into cracks.

23

Cloudless. Pink asters. Early cool before forecasted heat. Surely the last blurt of summer in late autumn. Evie balances her Light Fury (a white dragon) on the brush box branch hanging low above the 'play centre'—the girls' name for the gravestone they've come to build villages of flowers on (in honour of alicorns again), surrounded by that knee-high cast-iron fence (the FORCEFIELD).

Only the occasional small plane flies overhead, like a bee.

> *we tell ourselves that pestilence is a mere bogey of the mind, a bad dream that will pass away. But it doesn't always pass away and, from one bad dream to another, it is [we] who pass away ...*

I look up from my phone and Camus. Time to play.

Frankie finds us mid-hide-and-seek in the elms near the marble cross of Eliza Emily Donnithorne, the Newtown recluse who, it's said, was the inspiration for Dickens' Miss Havisham. Frankie and I linger with Donnithorne's ghost.

By the 1848 she-oaks, Tilda has given up on hide-and-seek to collect rocks.

24

I misread what's written on the hackberry tree: 'yr hot air is hurting my feelings' ('so hot ur hurting my feelings'). I lie on a gravestone in the sun, feel the warm scratch of baking sandstone.

'Daddy!' they scream in unison.

25

Turning and now not turning, both the girls' scooters' back wheels have come off their axles. *The centre cannot hold* … and out beyond the FORECFIELD, running in widening circles around the plinth I'm on, Frankie and the girls are each now out of sight, out of earshot, as I yell into the cemetery air.

The gravel driveway crunches its broken star shards beneath my feet, the same gravel that sent Evie and Tilda sprawling the other day, beneath the giant bamboo, the Moreton Bay Cthulhu and the line of Canary Island palms like massive spiky lollipops, all of them swaying, rustling, then headbanging in the wind as it picks up from somewhere deep in the ground-glass sky.

Notes

'Spleen 1' to 'Spleen 4' are loose translations of Charles Baudelaire's four different *Spleen* poems. 'Spleen 2' builds on the imagery of Sean Bonney's typewriter version. 'Hell I Copped' quotes former Australian Senator John Madigan: 'submarines are the spaceships of the ocean'. 'Beneath the Sparkle' misquotes articles by Jim O'Rourke in the *Daily Telegraph*, Brett Lackey and Charlie Croe in the *Daily Mail Australia*, and David Adams in *Pedestrian*. 'An Absolutely Ordinary Poem' is written after Mary Ruefle's 'A Certain Swirl', Les Murray's 'An Absolutely Ordinary Rainbow' and John Forbes' 'On the Beach: A Bicentennial Poem'. 'New Work Metaphorics' adapts received phrases from *God: An Itinerary* by Régis Debray. In 'Pink Sun', 'where the bloody hell are ya' references a $180m Tourism Australia ad campaign from 2006, when the current prime minister Scott Morrison was managing director of Tourism Australia. 'Captain's Cull' is formed entirely of the Twitter posts and quoted speech of Scott Morrison, but filtered through variations of the Oulipo N + 7 game. 'The Last Few Budgets in a Nutshell' misquotes Liberal Party budget speeches dating back to 2015. 'Sparkling Anxiety' adapts and collages phrases from Baudelaire's *Paris Spleen* prose poems throughout; there are also adapted phrases from the work of Sean Bonney, Ernst Bloch and Pam Brown; its title cites a meme that went viral on Twitter: 'It's only existentialism if it comes from the existentialism region of France. Otherwise, it's just sparkling anxiety.'

'27 Materialisations of Sydney Cloud' contains the phrase 'a total fucking gas' from 'Ode to Tropical Skiing' by John Forbes. '17 Great Dog Shits of Sydney' takes its inspiration from Brett Whiteley's painting *The Fifteen Great Dog Pisses of Paris*; the poem's first line is in fact a three-line poem called 'Flying' by Michael Dransfield, while the last line is a tweaked version of two lines by Elizabeth Riddell from her poem 'Suburban Song': 'Now all the dogs with folded paws / Stare at the lowering sky.' 'January 26' is written after Matthew Zapruder's '4th of July'. 'Planned Obsolescences' transmutes Guy Debord: 'What appears is good; what is good appears', Walter Benjamin: 'That things just go on is the catastrophe', and Jacques Lacan: 'The death drive is a nostalgia for lost harmony'. 'Morning Walks in a Time of Plague' relies on some history of Camperdown Cemetery found on *Wikipedia* and in *A Stroll Through the Historic Camperdown Cemetery, NSW* by P.W. Gledhill; all quotes of writers and musicians are acknowledged in-text; the translation of Boccaccio is by Richard Aldington; translations of Baudelaire are by Louise Varèse; translations of Camus are by Stuart Gilbert; and the translation of Reverdy is by John Ashbery. The epigraph is taken from Baudelaire's prose poem 'L'Étranger' ('The Stranger'), translated by Louise Varèse.

Acknowledgements

Sydney Spleen was written on unceded Gadigal land.

Poems included in this book have appeared in the following publications: *Australian Book Review*, *Australian Poetry Anthology 2020*, *Australian Poetry Journal*, Black Inc.'s *Best Australian Poems 2018*, *Buying Online: Newcastle Poetry Prize Anthology 2018*, *Cordite Poetry Review*, *Demos Journal*, *Island Magazine*, *Mascara Literary Review*, *Meanjin*, *Minarets*, *otoliths*, *Philament*, *Pink Cover Zine*, *Rabbit Poetry Journal*, *Red Room Poetry*, *Social Alternatives*, *Visual Verse*.

'Sparkling Anxiety' won the Charles Rischbieth Jury Poetry Prize 2020. 'King Tide' was highly commended in the Gwen Harwood Poetry Prize 2017 and shortlisted for the Newcastle Poetry Prize 2018. '27 Materialisations of Sydney Cloud' appeared in *Best Australian Poems 2018*.

The writing of this book has been assisted by the Australia Council for the Arts in the form of two literature grants, one for New Work (2016) and one from their Resilience Fund (2020).

Special thanks to Chris Edwards, Evelyn Araluen and Lisa Gorton for their editorial feedback on manuscripts of this book, and to Aleesha Paz and all at Giramondo.

Big love to Frankie, Evie and Tilda for being the sky in my life, and for seeing things I don't see. And to Minky, who won't be around for much longer. This book is dedicated to small black dogs everywhere.

About the author

After emigrating from London to Sydney at age three, Toby Fitch has lived on Gadigal land for thirty-six years, working as a poet, critic, teacher and editor. He is the current poetry editor of *Overland* and a sessional academic in creative writing at the University of Sydney. His books of poetry include *Rawshock*, which won the Grace Leven Prize for Poetry 2012; *Jerilderies*; *The Bloomin' Notions of Other & Beau*; *ILL LIT POP*; *Where Only the Sky had Hung Before*; and *Object Permanence: Selected Calligrammes*. *Sydney Spleen* is his seventh collection. He recently moved with his partner, two daughters and staffy from Newtown to Newcastle (Awabakal land).